Unraveled *roots*

Exposing the Hidden Causes
of Damaging Behaviors

KARIN BARBITO | MELINDA MEANS | LISA ROWE, LCSW
FOREWORD BY KATHY KOCH, PHD, PRESIDENT, CELEBRATE KIDS, INC.

Endorsements

How often have we heard the phrase, "we need to get to the 'root cause' of…"? In *Unraveled Roots: Exposing the Hidden Causes of Damaging Behaviors*, Karin, Melinda, and Lisa offer a well-thought-out roadmap – clearly **identifying and defining** four distinct root causes of wounds, and gently guiding the reader through healing and restoration from that woundedness. They write from their own journeys: "Healing comes in layers, and is risky… but as we heal, we become stronger." We all have wounds and we all need healing. You will have no doubt that they are walking with you and rooting for you on **your** journey to healing, wholeness, freedom, and greater joy. Take this journey with them. It's worth it, because you're worth it.

—Karen Garnett, Consultant, Culture of Life Network

Wanting to change and needing to change, but not being able to change, is painful. It's demoralizing. Hope becomes despair. Confusion. Embarrassment. Anger. Fear. I'm excited you haven't given up. I know you haven't because you're holding this book. I'm proud of you for wanting more for yourself . . . Changes in your beliefs and behaviors are possible, especially when you understand your past. You may be surprised to discover its power. It doesn't need to be the negative anchor it has perhaps been. With the help provided in these pages, you can reinterpret your past so it doesn't weigh you down. You can move on and discover new sources of beliefs and attitudes . . . I'm so glad you found this book.

—Kathy Koch, Ph.D., President, Celebrate Kids, Inc.

Dedication

We dedicate this book
to the roots of our past.
Thank you for creating in us
a desire for hope and healing.

Contents

Foreword

Before I traveled as much as I do now, I enjoyed growing African violets. Of course, to enjoy the pink, purple, and white blossoms, I had to take care of the plants by putting them in the right light and watering the soil. I had to pull off and throw away dead blossoms. I also had to pay attention and transfer plants to larger containers when they were no longer growing. This was a sign the roots were crowded. The beauty depended on what I could not see.

Now I only grow ordinary vines in vases full of water. There's no soil to dry up or crowded-out roots. I can have plants and still travel. Usually.

After being away from my home for a month, I got home to discover that several leaves had fallen from one of my vines. Enough water had evaporated and been used by the roots to mean some roots didn't have access to their source of life. Without roots functioning well, part of the vine withered, and leaves died. I was disappointed.

Roots don't just matter in plants. They matter in us. In a plant, the roots anchor the plants and absorb nutrients and moisture. For us, our past serves as an anchor and a significant source of beliefs and attitudes. Our past influences our future.

I'm so glad you found this book. Changes in your beliefs and behaviors are possible, especially when you understand your past. You may be surprised to discover its power. It doesn't need to be the negative anchor it has perhaps been. With the help provided in these pages, you can reinterpret your past so it doesn't weigh you down. You can move on and discover new sources of beliefs and attitudes.

For 30 years, I've been teaching and writing about the role our roots have on our fruit. Today does influence tomorrow. Childhood influences adulthood.

Who we are now has something to do with who we used to be. Absolutely! I have often talked about the need to kill the spider (the cause of our behavior) rather than just sweeping away the web (the behavior). This unraveled roots analogy is much stronger. No one is afraid of roots.

Have you been frustrated that change comes slowly or doesn't last? Perhaps, as I have often done, you have simply dusted the spider webs from the windowsill only to wake up the next day to discover they're back. Maybe you have pulled dead blossoms from plants thinking you'd never have to do that again.

If we want a beautiful life, we must dig deep. We must understand and accurately interpret our roots. Our history can't be changed, but we can learn to change what we think about it.

The truths here will help you untangle your thoughts about your past and the people and events that caused you to become who you are. Unraveling your roots will make your past clear. Your new understandings will change your perspective about yourself and those people and events from your past. Now your present and future can be different.

Wanting to change and needing to change, but not being able to change, is painful. It's demoralizing. Hope becomes despair. Confusion. Embarrassment. Anger. Fear. I'm excited you haven't given up. I know you haven't because you're holding this book. I'm proud of you for wanting more for yourself.

When I met Karin, Melinda, and Lisa, we quickly bonded. We finished each other's sentences as we discovered how closely aligned our beliefs were. These gifted women love well. They are trustworthy. They're committed to the God of the Bible. Their concerns for you and our culture inspire me. I'm proud to endorse their resource. I'll do everything I can to publicize it because there are too many people controlled by their past and they don't even know it. Digging up our roots and being planted in healthier soil of accurate understandings changes us.

I'm not surprised God uses a tree and roots analogy when sharing about people who trust in God in Jeremiah 17:7-8. Ultimately, this is what I pray for you. As you continue to journey in the life you have, may you choose to trust more in God. He will help you see your past accurately and with compassion. He will help you learn new beliefs, behaviors, and strategies going forward. I pray, because we learn to trust God, we are each "like a tree planted by water, that sends out its roots by the stream, and does not fear when heat comes, for its leaves remain green, and is not anxious in the year of drought, for it does not cease to bear fruit."

Kathy Koch, Ph.D.
Founder and President, Celebrate Kids, Inc.
Co-founder, Ignite the Family

Warning Label

Reading this book is risky. It's important for you to know that before you begin this journey. Walking out a new path, making different choices, is rarely safe or predictable. But nothing truly worth pursuing is without risk.

Our tendency can be to cling to well-worn patterns, mindsets, or behaviors even if they cause us pain. There's a strange sense of comfort in the familiar. At least we know what to expect. The outcomes of new choices can seem uncertain and far away. We may be afraid of how other people will react. They're often comfortable with our patterns, too. Healing rocks the boat. It shakes the tree.

Healing means exposure. We have to make ourselves vulnerable. Wounds can't be healed unless we begin to reveal them to trusted, loving people. Some wounds are so deeply buried beneath the surface that we don't even realize they are there. They lie dormant until something or someone pokes at the wound. And suddenly we're reliving an experience, a rejection, a season of difficulty that happened so long ago we may have forgotten it. Yet, the pain that unexpectedly rises to the surface is as real as if it had just occurred yesterday.

As I began writing this book, I thought of you and prayed often as I considered how challenging *reading* and processing this book could be *for you*.

But I didn't consider how difficult and painful *writing* this book would be *for me*. The famous poet Robert Frost once said, "No tears in the writer, no tears in the reader." In other words, the writer has to go to deep, painful places if he or she expects to inspire the reader to do the same. Tears come from a tender, vulnerable place that can't be easily accessed.

As I wrote, interviewed, and researched for this book, I had "a-ha" moments about the roots of some of my own choices, feelings, and behaviors. It brought me to a deeper level of healing, self-acceptance, and forgiveness and grace for others. It was simultaneously painful and freeing. I was grateful for those moments.

But about midway through the writing process, something happened that *shook my core*. The project unexpectedly went in a different direction that suddenly brought back memories of a very painful experience from my past—an experience that triggered deep wounds of rejection in me. Suddenly, I felt like I was being forced to go back to that place. And I didn't think I could. I certainly didn't want to. That place made me feel like I wasn't valuable, like I wasn't important. It made me feel like who I was and what I had to offer wasn't "enough."

For weeks, I had been putting my heart—pieces of who I am—on page after page. As I was writing one day, I raised my fingers off the keyboard. Suddenly, I thought: *I can't write one more word. What I'm doing isn't enough. And if this isn't enough—if who I am isn't enough—then I don't have anything else to offer.* I was certain that my role in this book was done.

That deep root of rejection didn't grow overnight. It was planted in me early and through a variety of sources and experiences. That's usually the case, isn't it?

Growing up, my family seemed normal, stable, and loving. My mother's quirky, fun personality kept life interesting. But so often I longed for her to be dependable and in control. I resented her undependability and emotional instability. It wasn't until I was an adult that she was diagnosed with bipolar disorder. All I knew growing up was that something seemed "off." Although I knew I was loved, a sense of loneliness marked my childhood. I felt an emotional distance with my mom that I couldn't seem to bridge no matter how hard I tried.

Extended family relationships were also complicated. My aunt and uncle raised my mother after my grandmother died suddenly. Until the day my mother passed away, my aunt never let my mom forget all the sacrifices she had made to raise her. It was a relationship characterized by guilt and manipulation. It was as if my aunt had convinced my mom that connecting with her own children was an act of disloyalty.

For different reasons, neither of my parents was willing or able to make the necessary emotional break from the people who raised them in order to be fully emotionally invested in each other and their children.

The turmoil and dysfunction in my home made me feel uncomfortable and out of control. I coped by trying to be the "good girl." Performance and people pleasing became my "drugs" of choice. I was looking to fill that deep need for stability, value, love, and acceptance.

As I got older, I gradually began to connect the dots behind some of my mother's behaviors and emotional disconnection. My grandparents married young; and my grandmother became pregnant right away. Under financial and family pressures, she chose abortion. My mom was born a few years later, but my grandparents divorced shortly after. When my mom was six, her mother, at the age of 26, died suddenly from a complication after surgery. My mother had only sporadic contact with her dad throughout her growing up years.

My mom brought all those wounds and feelings of abandonment, combined with an untreated mental illness, into her marriage and family. She was lonely, too. She wanted to connect with us, but I don't think she knew how.

After I got married, I found myself repeating so many of the same patterns I witnessed growing up. They just looked a little different. Parenting and healthy connection with my children were infinitely harder than I ever dreamed they would be. My marriage hit a long, difficult season. I longed for a happy family, to make things better, but I didn't know how. Everything I tried seemed to fail. Suddenly, my compassion for my mother began to grow by leaps and bounds. She did the best she could with the tools and level of healing she had—which wasn't much. I realized that she truly did *want* to connect more closely with me. Her own wounds, unresolved issues, and upbringing prevented her from knowing how.

My mom and I weren't so different after all.

Finally, gradually, I began to let go of *my* efforts to try to feel loved, to fix my life, and my family. And God began to patiently and lovingly show me a better way. New choices. New patterns. Ones that fit the way He made me. Healing comes in layers. We will never fully "arrive" on this healing journey. But as we make healthier choices, we get stronger. The pain of the past isn't gone, but it just doesn't define us anymore.

That painful experience from my past? I'm a different person now. I felt God speak to my heart: *You aren't who you were then. You don't have to react the same way. It can be different this time. You don't have to be afraid.*

Healing *is* risky. But you are valuable enough to take the gamble. Read on.

—Melinda Means

How to Use This Book

Because exploring old memories and past wounds will likely be difficult and painful at times, we highly recommend taking the journey through *Unraveled Roots* in a small group setting with a trained facilitator. However, if that is not possible, we encourage you to consider asking a trusted friend, counselor, or church leader to come alongside as you explore your past and discover a new healing path.

In a group setting, please be aware that everything that is shared should be kept strictly confidential and within the group. Your time together needs to feel safe so conversation can be positive, honest, and free flowing.

Throughout this book, you will find a discussion section called "Unravel the Root: Truth Story." These are real-life stories that relate to the root we are examining in each chapter. Through these stories, we walk you through the process of recognizing parallels of dysfunction in your own story and how to replace the lies and behaviors that stemmed from that root with truth and healthier choices.

Each of us has our own story. Some of our stories and wounds can seem more difficult or extreme than others. We invite and encourage you to refrain from judgments about others' experiences. No one should feel that their story is not important or that their wounds are not significant simply because they don't seem to be as intense as someone else's. Because of our temperaments and other factors, a seemingly less traumatic experience in someone else's life could actually be far more damaging than it seems.

Please be aware that we use the term "parent" throughout the book to encompass the person or persons who raised you, whether that is a guardian, grandparent, foster parent, or others.

You were on our minds long before this book was written, and as each chapter and story were formed. May your journey through *Unraveled Roots* lead you to health and healing.

For more information about finding or forming an *Unraveled Roots* group, please email info@unraveledroots.com.

Chapter One

Why Am I Here?

Every child has dreams. They are often secret hopes and wishes that he or she never verbalizes except maybe to a teddy bear or a trusted friend in a late night giggle session. When you're a child, the sky's the limit. Anything seems possible. Dreams are the things that fairy tales are made of.

No little girl ever dreams of becoming a prostitute, but she does.

No little boy ever dreams of beating his wife, but he does.

No man or woman ever dreams of one day aborting their child, but they do.

So many of us find ourselves living a life we never dreamed. Sometimes those childhood dreams get snuffed out through a single terrible, violent act or at such a young age that we struggle to remember them. For others of us, they are gradually, but heartbreakingly, extinguished through many disappointments and traumas over many years.

You want life to be different, but have no idea how to change it. You may doubt that change is even possible. But you're here because you're tired of the cycle. Tired of finding yourself in the same place over and over again. Life feels like a continuous and lonely battle; and you feel like you're losing the fight. In fact, you're not sure that you have any fight left in you. We're here to tell you this: *You are not alone.* You didn't arrive here overnight. And there is a reason you are in this place.

You are not alone. You didn't arrive here overnight. And there is a reason you are in this place.

Imagine a gardener who is growing a tree. In time, the tree begins to blossom and fruit begins to grow. One day, the gardener notices the fruit has spots and feels mushy. She bites into it and it doesn't taste good. She cuts off the bad fruit, hoping better fruit will grow. She pays special attention to the fruit and treats it with a variety of methods. She thinks that will solve the problem. However, when she goes out a few days later, new fruit has grown that is just as unhealthy as the fruit she'd tried so hard to get rid of. And the fruit she "treated" only continues to look worse. She begins to believe that growing good fruit is hopeless.

The "fruit" in our lives—the behaviors and choices we make—are often a reflection of deeper issues that lie beneath the surface. We can't see them, so we often focus on the fruit, but we always seem to experience the same bitter harvest: You may have tried hard to stay clean, but can't seem to break free from your addiction. Maybe you've left an abusive relationship, only to choose another man who abuses you. Or perhaps you vowed to never have another abortion, only to find yourself pregnant again and making the same choice.

The problem that is visible to the eye is always caused by what lies beneath the surface.

Here's what we often miss: The problem that is visible to the eye is always caused by what lies beneath the surface. Unhealthy and damaging fruit comes from diseased roots. *The roots feed the tree.* If the gardener tries to make the fruit better without treating the roots, she will be perpetually frustrated and the tree will grow sicker and sicker. Once the root problems are identified and addressed, the tree will gradually begin to produce good fruit.

Fruit from the family tree

Long before you ever found yourself in this place—long before you were even born—the seeds were planted. The roots had been steadily growing beneath the surface just waiting to tangle you up. We can usually find the "why" behind our choices and behavior when we take a careful and detailed examination of the generations before us.

Throughout this workbook, we will be leading you through a process of examining your choices and behaviors and relating them to the generations before you. Many ancestry websites provide a *genealogy*—revealing more about *who* is in your family tree. However, we are going to go much deeper than the "who." We will focus on helping you identify hidden patterns, behaviors, and significant events from past generations that may be impacting you today. For example, our father abandons us, so we find ourselves settling for a verbally or physically abusive boyfriend because we subconsciously feel that if our father doesn't want to be with us, he must not love us. If that's the case, we believe nobody else will love us either. So we go with whoever shows interest in us, even if it's hurtful or damaging.

Maybe we were sexually abused as a child and find ourselves choosing men who also use and abuse us. Or, we may have grown up in an outwardly healthy-looking family. But behind closed doors, that "healthy" mother or father was emotionally dis- **We need awareness to be able to begin to make different, healthier choices.** tant and/or verbally abusive, making it much more difficult for us to feel loved and form healthy relationships.

The bottom line is that we are often groomed from childhood for the behaviors and choices we are now making. We weren't equipped to make different choices. Sometimes the ones who set us up for this dysfunctional path did so consciously, but often, they are simply acting out of their own tangled roots. We all have choices. This *does not* absolve them of all responsibility for their choices, but it does help to explain them. However, regardless of what our parents did or didn't do, harboring resentment and bitterness towards them keeps us paralyzed in the past. As we begin to recognize our own mistakes, we have the opportunity to make healthier choices. We may not have had power to change what happened to us as a child, but we do have power over how we act and react as an adult.

We need awareness to be able to begin to make different, healthier choices. Unhealthy patterns of behavior are often deeply ingrained and seem normal to us. We don't even realize they are damaging. Until we get to the root of our patterns, we will stay in the dark to the truth and continue to make the same poor choices. It is when our eyes are opened that we can begin to forge a new, life-giving path.

There is a reason why you are here

There *is* a reason you are in this place of hurt and struggle. But there's also a reason you are in *this* place, reading *this* book during *this* time in your life, hoping and searching for an answer and a solution. You did not come here by accident. Yes, our upbringing and experiences have groomed us and normalized and solidified behaviors and unhealthy choices. But it's never too late to walk a new path. We are inviting you to take this journey with us. We encourage you to open your mind and heart to new possibilities—to dare to dream a little again.

Throughout this journey, we hope to answer the question, "Why am I *here*?" in more ways than one. As we've discussed, our goal is to open your eyes to the generational patterns that led you to this place so you can begin to make healthy choices. We want to help you discover the "why" behind your "what." But we also desire to open your eyes to the truth that you are here on this earth for a very important purpose. In fact, each of us was uniquely created with a purpose only we can fulfill. We want to partner with you as you discover, grow, and walk out your purpose.

Over the next four chapters, we will be exploring common "roots" of damaging choices. You may have heard of them, but never connected them to your own behaviors and circumstances. We may be redefining root issues in ways that you have never considered before. Or, perhaps you may not have even known one or more of these issues could lead to unhealthy behaviors. However, if none of these roots seem to fit your personal situation or experience, write your thoughts down and be sure to bring them up with your mentor, in your small group, or privately with your leader, if you feel that is more appropriate and comfortable for you.

As you read this book, you may begin to think of others who could benefit from this information. Even if you don't personally relate to all the roots mentioned, this book may help you to be a more compassionate friend. It may help you to better understand others in your life.

Throughout the book, we will be walking you through "Truth Stories." These are real-life stories that help illustrate the four roots that we are exploring. Through reading and examining others' experiences, you may begin to understand more about how your past shaped you and set you up for the choices you are now making. The goal is never to go back and assign blame. That is not productive and does nothing to move you forward. The goal is to go back and look at what shaped you so you can learn from it, understand the "why" behind those choices, start the forgiveness and healing process, and pass down a healthier legacy to your children.

We are privileged to walk alongside you in this healing journey.

We are glad you are *here*. You are not alone.

He heals the brokenhearted and binds up their wounds.

Psalms 147:3 (NIV)

Chapter Two

The Root of Abandonment

Young fruit trees are vulnerable. Careful attention is needed to make sure the tree has the proper balance of sunlight, water, and other nutrients. Vigilance is vital to nourish and protect it from pests and disease so it can grow to produce healthy, vibrant fruit. Different kinds of trees require different levels and types of nurturing, but they have one element in common: Their growth can't be left to chance. Tiny trees need a lot of love and attention to flourish.

Young humans are much the same way. Each of us requires a different and unique balance of care, support, and nurturing. But the common thread is this: We all need love, security, and connection to thrive. The very first connection that we are designed to make is with our parents. When that bond is healthy and close, it establishes a security in us as children that we are likely to carry into adulthood. It sets a model and foundation for forming stable and emotionally life-giving relationships and attachments as we grow. Secure attachment to our parent(s) helps provide a positive view of ourselves and gives us the confidence to branch out and explore the world around us.[1] We are also often more likely to be drawn to and form relationships with others who exhibit those same loving and beneficial qualities.

However, the opposite is also true. When that bond is damaged, unhealthy, or non-existent, we can often unconsciously carry the effects of that void into adulthood. The fruit of the root of abandonment—and We all need love, security, and connection to thrive.

the low self-worth that frequently results—can be a reluctance to commit to relationships because of fear of rejection. Or, we may find ourselves engaging in unhealthy attachments and behaviors in order to numb the pain and fill the internal or external sense of emptiness and loss.

The absence of a caretaker

When we think of abandonment, a physical absence is usually what comes to mind. One of the definitions of "abandon," according to Merriam-Webster Dictionary is "to withdraw protection, support, or help from."[2] The withdrawal of the physical presence of a parent can happen as a result of a divorce. A parent walks out on the family. In some cases, the relationship ceases right then and there. We have little or no contact from that day forward. In other cases, a connection still exists, but it is sporadic, undependable, or conditional based on the parent's whims or on our behavior. Maybe a close bond remains intact. However, nothing can change the fact that the parent's physical presence is no longer in the home. Even if a marriage or parent relationship ends because of verbal or physical abuse and the break is necessary and beneficial, it does not change the fact that the void of a parent is still deeply felt.

Knowing we're loved in our heads and feeling we're loved in our hearts are two very different things.

Perhaps one or both parents never walked *in*. We may have grown up in a single parent household and never had any relationship with the other parent. For a variety of reasons, others of us grew up in adoptive homes or in foster care. Some of us lost a parent during our childhood due to a tragic accident or disease or the result of substance abuse or other damaging behaviors. Regardless of the reason or who stepped in after the abandonment, the emptiness, feelings, and loss of attachment are the same. We crave the love and stability we were designed to have as an anchor. We need to acknowledge this loss. The remaining parent or caregiver may have done the very best he or she could. However, it often simply isn't enough to compensate for the love and stability we needed and were designed to have so we could grow and thrive in every area of our lives.

Alone in the forest

Have you ever been in a crowd of people and felt lonely? Misunderstood? Or simply invisible? We all have at one time or another. But perhaps some of us felt that for most of our childhood. Parents or other caregivers were physically present. Our basic needs for food and shelter were met. They may have told us they loved us, showed up for events, and even helped us go to college. By all external appearances, they were "good" parents. Yet, despite all that, we didn't feel emotionally *connected*. We didn't feel loved.

From our experience, we've seen this result for a number of reasons, including:

- We felt our feelings, needs, opinions, or accomplishments weren't acceptable, recognized, or valued.

- Home didn't feel like a safe place to push boundaries or make mistakes.

- We experienced verbal or emotional abuse. The parent(s) might have withheld love, affection, or approval. Or perhaps we were held to unwavering, impossible expectations that we could never meet no matter how hard we tried. We may have had an overall sense of parental disappointment in who we are as a person.

- We suffered physical and/or sexual abuse.

- We were raised by a parent or caregiver who struggled with mental health issues like depression.

- We were raised by a parent who had an addiction such as alcohol or gambling.

We might have never recognized some of these experiences as "abandonment." It may have just felt like an internal, gnawing, or profound sense of insecurity, disconnect, and loneliness that we couldn't quite identify. The sobering truth is that a caretaker can supply all the basic nutrients we need to survive without providing the full heart involvement we need to thrive. *Knowing* we're loved in our heads and *feeling* we're loved in our hearts are two very different things.

Unravel the Root
Michelle's Truth Story

Now let's identify and unravel the telltale signs of abandonment in a real-life story. As you read, keep in mind that we tend to either model what we've observed growing up or we make destructive, unhealthy choices to cope with the wounds that resulted from the root.

The details of "Michelle's" life will not exactly match yours. The goal is not to *compare* your experience to this one. Rather, we encourage you to *relate to* the loneliness, emotions, and other generational elements that may have been present in your own personal story.

State the Facts.

Michelle came for therapy only when she ran out of other options. She simply couldn't continue with her current lifestyle any longer. If she did, she would likely die. Since her teens, Michelle had been deeply involved in drugs and other dangerous behaviors. Broken, but brilliant, Michelle was perplexed about why she had made such a mess of her life. She told her counselor that she came from the "perfect family." They lived in a comfortable suburban neighborhood. She had a nice house. Her parents attended every school activity and sporting event. They went on great vacations to exciting places. All of her siblings were successful. But she was a train wreck. She never fit that "perfect" mold.

As the counselor began to dig deeper, some startling facts began to emerge. Michelle revealed that her mom and dad lived in separate parts of the house. Her dad relied heavily on prescription pain medications to treat a variety of medical conditions. She always thought he was simply doing what he had to do in order to cope. The emotional divide between her parents was something she had accepted as normal. That same physical and emotional divide existed in her own relationship with her parents. They never sat down together for meals. She spent a lot of time alone after school. Her dad couldn't work, so her mom supported the family financially and worked constantly. In pain and depressed, her dad often isolated himself in his room for long periods of time. Their interactions were often strained and he was easily irritated and impatient with Michelle. As she talked with her counselor, Michelle began to recognize that her father was an addict. She realized that feeding his addiction always took priority over his family.

She also began to grasp the fact that because her mom was not receiving the love and connection she craved from her husband (Michelle's dad), she turned to work to fill her need for value, bonding, and approval. Her mom spent long hours trying to please people outside of the house and was not worrying about what was happening inside of the home.

Michelle also experienced sexual abuse as a child. She didn't feel safe or comfortable talking to her parents about it because they weren't emotionally available. She didn't understand that at the time. Instead, she buried her pain and searched for emotional connection by engaging in a series of very unhealthy relationships throughout her life. Finally, as a teenager, she met a guy who offered her a way out of the discontentment she was feeling at home. She moved in with him and began her descent into drugs and alcohol. She thought he loved her, but he only wanted to use her.

The root of abandonment was woven all through Michelle's childhood, but she didn't recognize it because everybody went to bed in the same house every night. However, her inability to identify the root didn't make it any less real or damaging.

So why didn't her siblings make the same damaging choices that she did? We are all created so uniquely. As a result, children in the same family can react to the same circumstances very differently. Through therapy, Michelle realized that her siblings were also affected by the abandonment, but because of their temperaments, they coped in different ways that may have been less obvious and damaging than hers.

Let's review: From the outside, Michelle's home life growing up appeared stable. Her parents attended all of her activities. They went on vacations together. However, there was an emotional divide between Michelle and her parents. Her father was addicted to pain pills. Her mother was always working to support the family. She felt alone and unimportant.

Let's reflect: What facts of your life are similar to Michelle's?

What facts of your life are different?

In what ways can you relate to her experience?

Expose the Lie.

Now let's look at the story that Michelle wove around her facts: "We have this perfect family. We go on vacations together. They've been to every one of my games. Why didn't I turn out like my siblings? There's something wrong with *me*. I'm the black sheep."

Let's reflect: What was the story *you* wove around the facts of your childhood?

Acknowledge the Behavior.

Michelle looked to men who didn't love her in order to feel emotional connectedness. She turned to drugs, sex, and alcohol to numb the pain of not feeling loved and valued by her parents. She chased the "rush" of a new man, drug, or experience, but each one was just a temporary "fix." It didn't last. She was disappointed time and again, perpetuating and further deepening the emotional wound of abandonment.

Let's reflect: What damaging behaviors are you choosing to fill the void? (Examples: drugs, alcohol, manipulation, need for control, approval-seeking)

Embrace the Truth.

Through counseling, Michelle was able to begin to connect some dots in her family history. Michelle's paternal grandparents were divorced when her father was a child. When Michelle's grandfather left the marriage, he emotionally disconnected from his son. The grandfather was physically present for visits, but kept an emotional distance from Michelle's father and the other siblings, maybe to ease his own pain. Michelle began to realize that her father didn't know how to connect with her because he didn't have that connection with his own father growing up.

Her maternal grandparents also had a difficult relationship. Her grandfather was an alcoholic who could rarely hold down a job for more than a few months at a time. Her grandmother was the one who kept the household going financially and emotionally. That model was handed down to her mother, who repeated it in her own household, especially as her father's medical problems and addiction intensified.

Let's reflect: After reading this chapter and Michelle's story, what roots of abandonment, if any, do you recognize in your family history?

As you consider your parents' upbringing, how does it change your attitude toward them?

Through this new understanding of her family history, and intentional commitment to her healing, Michelle began to reject the lie that there is something wrong with who she is. She gradually began to believe that she is valuable and created for a purpose. There is a plan for her life. Her parents didn't abandon her because she wasn't valuable. It was a result of their own problems, baggage, and woundedness. She was able to see that her behaviors and choices were unhealthy, damaging and led her to chase the exact opposite of what she craved: love, stability, and connection.

Let's reflect: Through the healing process, Michelle identified the root, lie, and truth of her story. In the columns below, write the root, lie, and truth of your story of abandonment.

ROOT	LIE	TRUTH
Michelle was emotionally abandoned by her parents, due to their own issues of addiction and unavailability.	*Michelle believed she had a perfect family. Michelle believed she was not as good as her siblings. There was something wrong with her.*	*Michelle's parents didn't abandon her because of lack of value.* **Michelle does have value.**

Change your Choices.

You may have heard the phrase, "the truth will set you free." Now that you have greater insight regarding the truth about you and your story, you can make different choices. The root of abandonment may have poisoned your life, but you can choose to treat it. You can interrupt that cycle of dysfunction.

Let's reflect: What habits and behaviors stemming from abandonment do you need and want to change?

How are you going to respond differently when something triggers those feelings of loss or emptiness? (Example: *When I'm feeling sad or lonely, I turn to alcohol or a boyfriend to make me feel good about myself. Instead, I am going to reach out to a supportive friend or do a productive activity that I enjoy.*)

Choosing to Connect

As we've said before, the goal of this book is not to lay blame. Our parents modeled what they knew and reacted out of what they experienced in their own personal "Truth Stories." However, clearly, they may have often valued their needs, wants, and desires above ours. That is their *choice* and we're *not* letting them off the hook for that. But as we better understand the underlying roots of their choices and behaviors, as well as our own, it can help increase our compassion and forgiveness for them. And that is an important part of our physical, emotional, and spiritual health. It is freeing to know that we can choose to move forward and start a new chapter in our story regardless of whether they ever acknowledge or express remorse for their behavior in our past chapters.

No matter what the root of abandonment looked like for us, we often tell ourselves similar lies: We are not loved. We are not good enough. We are never going to measure up. Nobody is ever going to love us or want us. We are not worthy.

But now we know the truth: We *are* valuable. Our lives *do* matter. We *do* have purpose. We *are* worthy of love.

As we choose to make positive steps and changes that reflect that truth, we will begin to find the connection we've always craved.

Though my father and mother forsake me, the Lord will receive me.

Psalm 27:10 (NIV)

Keep Growing!
A seed of encouragement

My parents divorced when I was so little that I don't ever remember them being together. Although a recovering addict, my father remained present and involved in my life—until I was in elementary school. Then, seemingly overnight, he relapsed and dropped off the radar. His sudden absence left a huge hole in my heart. I also struggled to feel emotionally connected to my mother, who was busy working and keeping everything afloat. I was starving for love and attention. I didn't realize it at the time, but I began to try to satisfy that hunger for affection and approval by being the "good girl." When that didn't achieve the results I craved, I became the rebel. I found a group of fellow renegades who would accept me. Shortly after I turned 13, I also became sexually active as a way to feel loved and wanted.

As I got older, my relationship with my mother only became more strained and complicated. Determined to be free from the pain of the past, I left home in my early teens. By my late teens, I had given birth to one child and had two abortions. I didn't look back. I felt no regret. I made the choice to abort because it was the choice that seemed best at the time. I believed I had the right to make the best choice for me. I married my daughter's father, but we soon divorced. I think in some way I was trying to "fix" what I had no power to change in my relationship with my dad. I wanted to recreate that relationship, but with a different, happier ending.

I eventually got married to the man who is now my husband. But I was still repeating so many patterns of my past. They looked a little different; however, I was getting the same results. I was damaging my kids' view of themselves. I was trying to connect with them in unhealthy ways and enabling their damaging choices. I began to take a hard look at myself. *Why was I doing these things?* I began to work on my self-esteem by slowly letting go of unhealthy habits and creating better boundaries in my relationships. I was growing more confidence and acceptance for who I am. But I began to realize I couldn't continue to grow without more encouragement and support. I started attending a local church and developing a real relationship with God. I gradually began to experience the unchanging love of God the Father who is always there for me. My heart was beginning to heal.

As I got healthier, I began working in a job that counseled women recovering from trauma. One of the most painful moments for me was when I was talking to a co-worker who was graphically describing a client's abortion experience. Suddenly, for the first time, I was struck by the devastating impact of my choice to abort. It was a turning point for me. Eventually, I went through an abortion healing experience provided by Support After Abortion, facilitated by Karin Barbito. This was another pivotal healing milestone for me. My husband attended the last group session with me and we both grieved my abortions together.

A huge motivator to keep going through the pain of healing and growing is seeing the positive effects on my marriage and children. As I make myself vulnerable, confess my mistakes and ask for their forgiveness at times, I increasingly establish new levels of intimacy with them. I am setting a healthier pattern for them to follow and pass down to their children.

—A former Support After Abortion client

Chapter Three

The Root of Addiction

Few living things are more exposed to the elements than trees. Out in the open, they experience a fierce combination of wind, rain, sleet, snow, and blazing heat. Yet despite it all, mature trees stand strong due to their natural ability to adapt. Harsh conditions actually cause them to grow even stronger.

People, on the other hand, have more difficulty weathering the unpredictable, constantly changing seasons of life. We don't automatically know our strength, value, and

From the time we're born, we look to our parents to answer some important questions for us.

purpose in life. It takes time, loving guidance, and experience for us to know who we are and how to handle challenging people and changing circumstances. From the time we're born, we look to our parents to answer some important questions for us: *Am I valuable? How do I respond when life gets stressful? How do I form friendships and relationships?*

Parents who struggle with substance or behavior addictions model unhealthy and damaging ways for their children to feel good about themselves, cope with disappointments, and build relationships. They reach for drugs, sex, food, or other things to make them feel happy, loved, in control—or at least to numb their pain. The result is that their method(s) of escaping pain, inflicted pain on *you*. It left you exposed to life's difficulties without healthy tools to help you learn, adapt, and grow stronger from them. As a result, you may have also adopted addictive behaviors.

The storm inside

No one ever sets out to become an addict. Your parent(s) may have begun to use certain substances or behaviors because they craved a temporary, pleasurable feeling, to escape from reality, or to soothe unpleasant emotions. Some can engage in these activities without ever becoming addicted. However, because of a variety of factors, other people are more vulnerable to becoming increasingly dependent on certain behaviors in order to cope and function.

Substance use disorder actually changes the brain's wiring over time. It causes intense cravings and makes it hard to stop using the substance. The more a person uses, the more he or she builds up a tolerance. He or she needs more and more of it to feel the same effects.[1]

Substances people can become addicted to include the following:[2]

- Alcohol
- Marijuana
- PCP, LSD and other hallucinogens
- Inhalants
- Opioid pain killers
- Sedatives, hypnotics and medications for anxiety
- Cocaine
- Methamphetamine
- Tobacco

People can also become addicted to behaviors, such as gambling or sex. These follow the same pattern as substance addictions and can have many of the same effects, including negative impacts on work, school and relationships and an increasing dependence despite the personal, mental, or physical harm it is inflicting.[3] Although only gambling disorder is officially recognized as a behavioral addiction by the DSM-5 (the leading diagnostic guide for mental health professionals), **many healthcare providers believe a variety of behaviors can also become addictions. These include:[4]**

- Shopping
- Pornography
- Video Games
- Internet
- Gambling
- Food
- Sex
- Exercise

The list of substances and behaviors that a person can become addicted to is endless. However, we are going to briefly explore three that we often see in the women we counsel and how your exposure to them as a child may still be affecting you today:

Substances

Substance abuse can manifest itself in a variety of ways—through alcohol, illegal substances, prescription drugs, or using legal substances improperly.[5] Some substance abusers are able to hide their addiction. They hold jobs, pay the bills, and interact reasonably well with the outside world. If that was the case in your home, you probably couldn't put it into words as a child, but you sensed something wasn't right. A lack of stability and trust tainted the relationship. You may have known you were loved, but you didn't feel loved. You may not have felt important to your parent(s). No one may have ever talked about it.[6] When you did try to ask questions, you may have been dismissed or made to feel like your feelings were unreasonable, disloyal, or misplaced. You may have been told that what you were experiencing (seeing, feeling, sensing) wasn't true. It may have been too hurtful to your sober parent for you to talk about the addicted parent. So you may begin to believe you can't trust that voice inside of you—the one that's telling you what's right or wrong.

Even if the problem was too obvious to deny, you may have been told not to tell, leaving you with no place to process your pain and emotions. Maybe it was a sibling or other close family member who was abusing substances— and not your parent(s). Still, your parents may have poured much of their energy and attention into that relative, leaving you feeling unimportant or without needed guidance, recognition, and support.

Substance abuse by a parent increases your risk for abusing substances.[7] Other effects of growing up with a parent who abused substances might be less visible or easy to connect to your past, including depression, anxiety, "numbing out" to emotional pain, acting out sexually, difficulty trusting others, staying engaged, and receiving and internalizing love and care from others.[8]

Sex

Sex was designed to be pleasurable. However, like any good thing, sex can be distorted and misused. Compulsive sexual behaviors can present in a variety of forms and degrees of severity, but can include compulsive masturbation, excessive use of pornography and repeated engagement in extramarital affairs.[9] In our experience, this could also include high-risk behaviors, such as numerous sexual partners or group sex.

Access to pornography has dramatically increased in the last 20 years with the growing use of the Internet. This means that it is more accessible to people than ever before. Early exposure to sexual content in the media may profoundly impact a child's values, attitudes, and behaviors toward sex and relationships.[10]

Healthy, intimate relationships are not just about sex. They also involve our thoughts and emotions. Healthy relationships are difficult at times, but they're built on respect for each other; partners are open and honest with one another without being cruel. The struggles and sacrifices help both partners to grow and bond in positive ways.

Healthy, intimate relationships are not just about sex. They're built on respect for each other.

Pornography, on the other hand, is fantasy. Pornography is "the depiction of erotic behavior (as in pictures or writing) intended to cause sexual excitement."[11] No real-life relationship can live up to it because it isn't real. It's not about getting to know or value the other person. It is purely about filling that person's immediate craving without commitment. Pornography makes the person an "object." The other person feels they can never please their spouse or partner because they can't live up to the idealized, perfect, airbrushed images on the Internet.

When children are exposed to pornographic images and sexual activities while their emotions, brains, and views of sex are still developing, they can become confused. That confusion about healthy sexual relationships can make a child more vulnerable. Other potential effects include depression, social anxiety, pre-mature sexual interactions with peers, self-harm, suicidal thoughts, or attempts, and other high-risk behaviors.[12]

Infidelity, whether it's with one other person or many, can shatter a child's confidence in their parents.

Addiction to sexual activities can flow from an insatiable desire for excitement or the "forbidden fruit"—the person or activity you "can't" have. Infidelity, whether it's with one other person or many, can shatter a child's confidence in their parents. A child may have assumed there was honesty between mom and dad that did not exist. When infidelity between them is exposed, the child may begin to ask themselves, *If my parents weren't honest with each other, how can I know they are being honest with* me? A child may begin to doubt if they can really trust the foundation of their relationships: *I thought my parents' relationship was real, but look what happened. I was wrong. What and who can I trust?*[13]

If your parent was a sex addict or you were exposed to sexual behaviors as a child, you may have developed a cynical view of marriage and relationships. You may believe that honesty and long-term commitment isn't possible, normal, desirable, or to be expected. Although you desire a healthy, long-term relationship, you may have no idea what that looks like or how to pursue one.

Food

One of the most basic needs we have as humans is food. While food is required to survive and was intended to provide pleasure, for some it becomes an unhealthy way to seek comfort or gain control in their lives.

Although many experts distinguish food addiction from eating disorders, such as anorexia, bulimia, or binge eating disorder,[14] the common thread is that parents who engage in compulsive food behaviors, such as overeating, food deprivation, or binging and purging, hand down an unhealthy view and model of eating to their children. Their example may have taught you that these food behaviors are an acceptable method of coping with disappointments and seeking comfort or control.

The damage can be done through the example the parent sets by their compulsive or unhealthy behaviors in regard to their own wellbeing. He or she may have also placed an overemphasis on controlling *your* food intake and weight as well, either subtly or overtly implying your appearance is not acceptable and doesn't measure up to their or society's standards. Or, the pressure you felt might not have been from your parents, but from the world's often unrealistic standards and harsh, cruel assessments of beauty and weight.

Why am I an addict?

Clearly, being exposed to addiction as a child can affect us in profound ways, including becoming an addict ourselves. But maybe you're thinking, *Addiction wasn't present in my home. Why am I struggling with it?* You don't have to have a parent with an addiction to be vulnerable to addiction yourself.

As we discussed in previous chapters, other childhood roots, such as abuse or abandonment, can also leave you feeling insecure, lonely, and worthless. You didn't receive the security, value, and love you needed as a child, so you became vulnerable to grasping at different, often damaging, ways to fill those empty, hurting places. You began to try to fill your need for love or control wherever you could find it. Then one day, you realized you're an addict: a slave to the very substances or behaviors that you believed would bring you love, value, and happiness.

Unravel the Root
Rebecca's Truth Story

State the facts.

Spirited, yet guarded, Rebecca was a young woman living a reckless existence. She was using drugs and alcohol heavily and engaging in high-risk sexual behaviors. She suffered from low self-esteem, as well as chronic bouts of depression and anxiety. She felt adrift and was desperate for an anchor. When the pain became too great for her to handle alone anymore, Rebecca finally turned to counseling and also found support at a local church.

Unraveling the roots of Rebecca's past provided insight into her behavior. Rebecca's parents divorced when she was very young. For several months after the divorce, Rebecca lived with her dad and had little contact with her mom. She remembers thinking: *My own mom doesn't even want to see me.* Although she lived primarily with her mom until she reached high school, Rebecca often felt emotionally disconnected from both her parents. Until her early teens, Rebecca was unaware her dad had a substance abuse problem. All she knew was that he wasn't engaged in her life. He expressed little affection and placed no boundaries on her activities or behavior. He seemed oddly afraid of enforcing any kind of discipline on her or her siblings.

Through counseling, Rebecca began to understand that because her maternal grandfather was an alcoholic, it led to her mom "literally marrying exactly the same kind of person her dad was. It was what seemed 'normal' to her. Then after my mom left my dad, she ended up marrying another alcoholic." Rebecca recognized that her mom was an enabler, trying to "fix" in her two husbands what she could never fix in her own dad as a child. She realized her mom's biggest fear was being alone and so she poured all her energy into the men in her life, turning a blind eye to what her behavior was doing to herself and her children. This left Rebecca with the primary task of taking care of her siblings.

Rebecca came to realize that her dad chose to be a "closet drinker" because *his* dad was a violent drunk. He didn't want his children to see him drunk. She now also realizes that her father's disconnection and reluctance to discipline was because his father abused him as a child. He was afraid he might repeat that same pattern with his own kids.

Even though she saw how destructive alcohol was in her family, Rebecca became a substance abuser herself: It was how she was taught to cope with life's problems. She saw how her loneliness and craving for male attention led her to engage in a string of short-term sexual relationships, even though they were unsatisfying and temporary. She didn't know how to form healthy relationships because she felt that everyone she ever depended on had let her down.

Now an adult, and after years of estrangement, Rebecca and her mom are both engaged in counseling and slowly talking through some of the painful aspects of their childhoods. They are finding healing as they expose the lies. Forgiveness, closeness, and understanding are gradually developing between them. Rebecca and her dad are also working toward mending their relationship.

Let's review: Although she didn't realize it until adolescence, Rebecca's dad was an alcoholic. Rebecca felt disconnected from her parents due to their lack of involvement in her life. She struggled with feelings of worthlessness and an inability to trust others, leading her to use drugs, sex, and alcohol to numb the pain from her childhood.

Let's reflect: Do you see any similarities between Rebecca's upbringing and your own?

How did your upbringing or reactions differ from hers?

How do you feel about your own Truth Story?

Expose the lie.

Now let's look at the story that Rebecca wove around her facts: "My parents don't care about me or what I'm doing. They aren't interested in my life. I'm not lovable and I can't depend on anyone but myself."

Let's reflect: If addiction was part of your childhood, what things did you tell yourself based on the behaviors you were witnessing?

Acknowledge the behavior.

Rebecca used drugs and alcohol because they were the only ways she knew how to cope with the pain and chaos in her internal and external worlds. She turned to sex to find the love and connection she didn't experience with her dad.

Let's reflect: What insight does this give you as you consider some of your own behaviors and choices?

Embrace the truth.

Rebecca came to realize that her mom married someone very much like her own father. Rebecca also saw how her father's disconnection was at least partly related to his own damaging and painful experiences as a child.

In other words, Rebecca's mom and dad repeated the patterns handed down to them. They were busy numbing their pain and trying to fill their own unmet needs. In her father's case, he also thought his distance was for Rebecca's protection. As she was able to realize this, it gave her more compassion for her parents. It opened the door for forgiveness and a level of understanding, without excusing the choices that they made and the pain they caused.

Let's reflect: After reading this chapter and Rebecca's story, what roots of addiction, if any, do you recognize in your family history?

Rebecca now realizes that her parents' disconnection with each other and with her was not because she wasn't lovable. She now knows she *is* valuable. She doesn't have to try to seek attention and find that value in unhealthy relationships. The truth of her parents' roots shattered Rebecca's belief that her parents didn't love her because she was not good enough or not worthy of their love. Now Rebecca no longer has to numb the pain of those lies with drugs and alcohol.

Let's reflect: As she began to heal, Rebecca was able to identify the root, lie and truth of her story. In the columns below, write the root, lie, and truth of your story as it relates to addiction.

ROOT	LIE	TRUTH
Rebecca's parents divorced when she was young. Rebecca felt an emotional disconnection from both parents.	*Rebecca believed that her parents didn't care about her or what she was doing. Rebecca was not lovable.*	*Rebecca's parents' disconnection from her was related to their own painful childhood experiences.* ***Rebecca is lovable.***

Change your choices.

Through counseling, her church and ongoing support systems, Rebecca was gradually able to replace drugs and alcohol with healthier tools that are allowing her to thrive in life's ever-changing climate.

Let's reflect: What habits and behaviors rooted in addiction do you need and want to change?

How are you going to respond differently when you want to turn to sex, drugs, or alcohol?

Coming out of the woods

Home is supposed to be our safe haven from the chaos. The place we can go to find respite from the storms of life. Living with an addict is often tense, chaotic, and unpredictable: Home is *not* a haven. The person or persons who were supposed to be your protector and guide left you exposed.

Growing up with an addict can make you feel like you're lost in a forest. Enveloped by darkness, you feel scared, powerless, and alone. If you're an adult, you *do* have power. You *don't* have to stay in that place. If you're a teen, you aren't powerless either. Tell another trusted adult, perhaps a friend's parent, a teacher, or counselor at school, about what you are experiencing and ask for their help.

So how do you get out of the forest? One step at a time. But which way is out? Now that the lie has been exposed, the truth embraced, and the root of your behaviors has been revealed, you'll gradually begin to make different choices.

No matter what you've been told or how you felt as a child, you can now embrace the truth that Christopher Robin—another frequent forest dweller—offered to his pal Winnie the Pooh: "You are braver than you believe, stronger than you seem, and smarter than you think."[15]

Now go walk it out, one step at a time.

For I am the Lord your God who takes hold of your right hand
and says to you, Do not fear; I will help you.

Isaiah 41:13 (NIV)

Keep Growing!

A seed of encouragement

Emotions may overwhelm you at times throughout this process. You may have abused drugs, alcohol, and engaged in dysfunctional relationships to numb your pain. As you begin to make better choices and distance yourself from these unhealthy ways of coping, you may begin to feel the impact of traumatic memories and emotions that you've numbed for months, years, or decades. It will make you want to give up. *Don't do it.* You will grow and find freedom through the pain that comes with healing. Your life can be different. How do I know? Because I've grown as I've pushed through the pain, time and time again, and increasingly experienced freedom. Because my life *is* different.

I coped with the pain of my past by numbing it through drugs and alcohol. I tried to satisfy my deeply felt need to be loved through sex with men who didn't truly care about me. Eventually, I decided getting married was the answer. A marriage based on all the wrong things and for all the wrong reasons is never a good idea. As our relationship simultaneously exploded and imploded and my addictions raged, I realized I simply couldn't live this way anymore. I wanted to live a different life, but I didn't know how. Still, I knew I was facing either prison or death if I continued on this path. So I made the choice to get clean. Recovering from drugs and alcohol was really hard. I just had to white-knuckle it through one emotional episode at a time. I can remember the first really tough time I had. I was in inpatient recovery and everything in me wanted to leave. I was like a caged animal, pacing back and forth. A war was raging inside me. I knew if I left I would use again. Part of me wanted that. A bigger part of me did not. I stayed: Victory #1.

I can remember another time that was incredibly hard. Someone suggested that I take a look into codependency to see if it was something that might be contributing to my struggles. I simply read the definition of "codependency" and literally cried for days. It was so confronting, so *me*. I thought I might be the first person to ever die from crying too much. Working through my codependency was one of the best things I've ever done—grueling, but worth every tear.

Each episode in the recovery process gets a little easier. I promise. The times when you are grieving and in pain get shorter and further apart. As you seek appropriate help and support* and begin the process of healing from your own past behaviors and choices, you can begin to see more clearly the pain you may have caused others. You'll start to take responsibility and make amends for your actions when appropriate. You aren't the person you used to be. You've drawn a line in the sand and said, "No more." You don't have to be ashamed of what was, because you can be very proud of who you are becoming.

—Karin Barbito

* See the Resources section on page 79.

Chapter Four

The Root of Abuse

One day, a gardener plants a young fruit tree. Although tiny, it shows great promise to produce good fruit. But then a violent storm comes up. The raging wind and rain savagely bends the vulnerable little tree and snaps some of its branches. The gardener doesn't blame the *tree* for its injured condition. He recognizes that it was the *storm* that caused the damage.

For many of us, the storm of abuse swept into our lives and broke something inside of us. Sadly we may have blamed ourselves:

> *I felt I was worth nothing so I let people treat me like nothing.*

> *I didn't feel like I could tell anyone. I was so ashamed. I had so much fear.*

> *For most of my life, I felt crazy and disconnected. I craved connection, but I was afraid to get close to people.*

> *I still become panicked and feel trapped when someone asks me to do something I can't do. For years, I didn't know why.*

Those are all actual quotes from women who experienced some form of childhood physical, emotional, sexual, and/or religious abuse. Do any of these statements sound like something *you* have said or thought? Have you wondered why you've always been plagued with such intense feelings of fear, isolation, and shame? So did these women.

In every case, they wondered why they felt so different and isolated from those around them. They didn't connect those feelings—and the choices that stemmed from them—to their early episodes of abuse. In fact, some of their memories were so traumatic and deeply buried that they didn't emerge until much later in life. These women were trying to relieve pain they often couldn't identify. They didn't realize that their life choices were actually further deepening their pain. Each woman believed that something was wrong with her at the very core of her being. One woman explained it this way: "I believed I was a mistake. I believed everything about me was a mistake."

Any kind of abuse, especially in childhood, can damage our sense of who we are and rob us of our security. As we've discussed in past chapters, roots are almost always intertwined. Children who have experienced abuse have also often been affected by other factors such as abandonment, substance abuse, and domestic violence. Each factor compounds the impact. Other factors can also influence the depth of the impact on a child, including the length and severity of the abuse and the nature of the relationship between the child and the abuser.

Even if you were not the direct object of abuse, witnessing or watching the dynamics of an abusive relationship in the home can also be extremely devastating. It can increase a child's risk for long-term physical and mental health conditions.[1]

Who can I trust?

Our ability to trust begins to form in childhood. We enter the world completely vulnerable. Trustworthy parents and caregivers provide our security and stability. If some of our earliest experiences were a betrayal of trust by the very people who were supposed to protect us, we struggle with our own value and how and who to trust.

Any kind of abuse, especially in childhood, can damage our sense of who we are and rob us of our security.

Emotional abuse can take a variety of forms, including name calling; rejection of the child's worth; bullying; isolating, and ignoring the child; and/or over-pressuring the child to behave and perform in ways that are far beyond the child's capabilities.[2] This form of abuse can be as much or more devastating as physical abuse. Language and emotions are powerful. If they are used as weapons, they can critically damage how we think and feel about others and ourselves. It's through the language we hear that we form our views about ourselves. Demeaning and insulting words embed themselves in our hearts and minds. We absorb them and identify ourselves by those labels such as ugly, fat, stupid, lazy, or worthless.

Patterns of damaging interactions between parent and child can create long-term effects, including depression, suicidal thoughts, learning difficulties, low self-esteem, anxiety symptoms, poor adult health, and difficulties with social skills and relationships.[3]

Both emotional and physical abuse are often rooted in the need to control another person.

While emotional abuse does not always lead to physical violence, physical violence *does not* occur without emotional abuse. Experts have differing viewpoints about what defines **physical abuse**, however, according to the World Health Organization, physical abuse of a child is defined as the intentional use of physical force against a child that results in – or has a high likelihood of resulting in – harm for the child's health, survival, development, or dignity. This includes hitting, beating, kicking, shaking, biting, strangling, scalding, burning, poisoning, and suffocating. Much physical violence against children in the home is inflicted with the object of punishing.[4]

Both emotional and physical abuse are often rooted in the need to control another person. A parent who was abused as a child can often repeat those same violent tendencies. In some cases, they might not even recognize that their behavior is abusive. A father or mother who grabs and uncontrollably screams at her child is often simply repeating the pattern set by his or her parent(s). Although damaging, it seems "normal" to them because that was their childhood experience and model.

In other cases—through no fault of your own—you may have become your parent's outlet to vent his or her pent-up rage for the abuse and lack of control he or she had as a child. Or, as we saw in Rebecca's story in the last chapter, abuse as a child can cause a parent to go to the other extreme.

Rebecca's father disconnected emotionally and didn't discipline her and her siblings because he feared he would repeat his own father's abusive patterns.

We can make choices that stem from "forgotten" abuse.

How a child reacts to abuse can depend upon a variety of factors, including the child's temperament, emotional makeup, and the severity and duration of the abuse. In some cases, the child blames himself or herself for the abuse. They believe if they just behaved better or tried harder, the violence or emotional abuse wouldn't have occurred: "If I didn't scream at my sister, my dad wouldn't have hit me."

Some children become incredibly withdrawn and passive. Others grow extremely angry and rebel against the parent(s) who are abusing them. Children may want to hurt their parents or harm others, so that others will feel the same kind of pain they do.

Sexual abuse is another form of physical abuse. Sexual abuse is unwanted sexual activity, with perpetrators using force, making threats, or taking advantage of victims not able to give consent.[5] So often, victims of sexual abuse feel shame. They may feel they invited it somehow. The body's sexual response can be involuntary at times. The body can enjoy and respond to certain sensations, even when the mind and emotions are repulsed and traumatized by it.

> "As a child, I was verbally abused by my dad. My mom didn't protect me. Then, my older brother began to show me inappropriate affection—fondling and other inappropriate touching. Even though I knew it was wrong, I was so damaged and hungry for love and acceptance that a part of me enjoyed it. I finally felt loved. It filled a void and a deep need in me."

—Rhonda, sexual abuse survivor

Often there is dissociation from the abuse. The mind protects us from things that are too painful for us to process emotionally. While the mind may block it from our present conscious memory, we can still unconsciously be making choices that stem from that "forgotten" abuse.

Seeds of trust

We've covered the more obvious kinds of abuse: physical, sexual, and emotional. Although often less acknowledged and discussed, experiencing religious abuse as a child can also be devastating. We were designed to have a healthy, loving  **Abuse, regardless of its form, chips away at our identity and security.** relationship with God. Unfortunately, sometimes parents and others can manipulate, shame, control, and intimidate us by using a false or distorted view of God and religion. They may use religion as a justification for abusive behaviors. This is not limited to a specific religion or denomination.

What is religious abuse? In our experience, the following characteristics are often present:

- The child is not allowed to question the family's beliefs and behaviors.

- The child is forced to isolate from others who do not share the parent's family's beliefs (an "us" vs. "them" mentality).

- The child is forced, manipulated, or subjected to abusive behaviors in the name of religion, often using fear, guilt, and shame.

In addition, profound confusion can occur if you grew up being taught religious values that were very different from how your parents behaved. This mixed message, or example of hypocrisy, can cause you to feel distant, resentful, or angry toward God or your faith.

> "My father always had a prominent role in the church, but behind closed doors, he was an angry, intimidating, brutal man. My fear of him continued throughout my life. My view of God was difficult to separate from my experiences with my parents. This abuse and insecurity has caused lack of trust and isolation. The roots of abuse ran through all

areas of my life. Over the years, it brought much emotional pain.

Growing up, I was incredibly insecure about my appearance and identity. When puberty hit, I became extremely busty. Instead of making me feel more confident, it made me feel even more uncomfortable about how I looked. It also opened the door for more abuse. My parents raised money for (religious) charities by standing outside businesses, asking for donations. Sometimes they would send me into bars to use my 'assets' to get money from drunken men. I wasn't more than 11 or 12 years old. They were driven to raise money, not by compassion, but for the awards and recognition they would get from the community.

Eventually, I discovered God to be very different than what had been portrayed to me growing up. My ongoing healing came through reading, Christian retreats, counseling and eventually attending seminary. God also provided amazing resources and highly qualified, discerning people to walk with me on my healing journey. I am also thankful for medication and advancements in medical science's understanding of post-traumatic stress disorder (PTSD)."

—Marie, religious and sexual abuse survivor

Abuse, regardless of its form, chips away at our identity and security. These are the building blocks necessary to make healthy, life-giving choices.

Unravel the Root
Lily's Truth Story

State the facts.

As a teenager, Lily began seriously considering taking her own life. She had a secret battle with lust, but she didn't know why. Shame pervaded her every thought and action. Her sense of self-loathing had become so deep and dark that she believed suicide was the only way to escape her overwhelming emotional pain. She told no one about her feelings. It didn't feel safe. Around this time, Lily's best friend and her mom began attending church. Lily went to church with them. She learned about God and discovered a hope, acceptance, and value she had never experienced before. Lily decided that life was worth living.

She was doing relatively well until her senior year in college when she came across a magazine article about sexual abuse. Lily became upset, disgusted, and angry. She couldn't understand her feelings or why the article was affecting her so deeply. She prayed and asked God to reveal to her why she was responding this way. One by one, the memories of years of sexual abuse, starting at age three, came to the surface. She felt physically ill and sobbed for days. For the first time, she revealed her secret to her best friend. Her friend listened with compassion as Lily recalled the memories that she had buried for so long.

Suddenly, it became clear to her why she struggled so much with feelings of shame and worthlessness. Her healing journey had begun, but more pain lurked beneath the surface. She felt safe enough to enter a relationship with a loving man who she thought she would marry, but one day he unexpectedly told her it was over. Her hidden insecurities and struggle with self-worth raged again. She developed an eating disorder and wasted away to a mere 78 pounds.

She knew she couldn't continue this way. So she spent an entire year focusing on becoming emotionally, physically, and spiritually healthy. Loving, supportive friends and a great counselor walked her through her pain. Although she still doesn't fully understand why the abuse happened to her, she realized that the abuse was not about her or anything she had done. It was the man's choice; and he chose to do something to her that was terrible. Instead of becoming bitter, she decided she was going to allow God and others into her pain. The healing that resulted allowed her to forgive her abuser, an act that gave her a measure of freedom and control that she didn't have as a child.

Lily is no longer tied to her abuser. She learned how to trust again, married a kind man, and raised two children. Memories of the abuse no longer control her life and decisions.

Let's review: Lily was sexually abused as a young child. To handle the pain, she deeply buried her memories of abuse—until the day reading a magazine article unexpectedly brought them to the surface. For years, she struggled with deep feelings of shame, insecurity, and guilt that led to suicidal thoughts and an eating disorder.

Let's reflect: What facts in your story are similar to Lily's?

How does your story differ from Lily's?

How can you relate to her feelings even if your facts are different?

Expose the lie.

Now let's look at the story that Lily wove around her facts: "I can't reveal my struggles with anyone. I am a shameful, worthless person. Life is so painful that suicide is my only option for relieving the anguish."

Let's reflect: If abuse was part of your childhood, what things did you tell yourself based on the behaviors you endured?

Acknowledge the behavior.

Lily began to understand that her eating disorder and thoughts of suicide were her attempt to stop the pain stemming from the abuse, and gave her a sense of control that she didn't have as a young child.

Let's reflect: What insight does this give you as you consider some of your own behaviors and choices?

Embrace the truth.

Lily came to realize that her identity (who she is) was badly damaged by early childhood sexual abuse. It caused her to feel shame about who she is as a person. Because she kept the abuse secret, she felt bound to her abuser by a sick form of intimacy, long after the abuse had ended. It prevented her from feeling safe and valuable enough to be known by others. That long buried pain and shame finally led to her desire to end her life.

Let's reflect: After reading this chapter and Lily's story, what roots of abuse, if any, do you recognize in your childhood history?

Once the secrecy was broken, Lily felt a weight was lifted. She was able to then process her pain with God, supportive counselors, and loving people. She understood that the abuse was not her fault. It was a part of her story, but it didn't define who she is. That healing allowed her to forgive her abuser, while not excusing or minimizing what he had done.

Let's reflect: As Lily experienced healing, she was able to identify the root, lie, and truth of her story. Below, write the root, lie, and truth of your story of abuse.

ROOT	LIE	TRUTH
At a very young age, Lily was sexually abused. Lily told no one about the abuse. Lily suppressed the pain of those memories for her protection.	*Lily couldn't reveal the abuse to anyone. Lily believed she was a shameful, worthless person. Lily believed suicide was her only option.*	*The abuse was not Lily's fault. Lily deserved to be protected. Abuse is part of Lily's story, but it does not define who she is. **Lily has immense worth.***

Change the behavior.

Lily's decision to break the isolation of keeping secrets was the first step in her healing. Her continued focus on her physical, spiritual, and emotional well-being by reaching out to God, friends, and counselors diminished her need for unhealthy ways of coping with her pain and her need to control.

Let's reflect: What habits and behaviors rooted in abuse do you need and want to change?

What is one step you can take *right now* to reach out for help?

Bent, but not broken

During an intense storm, a tree can be badly bent, especially if it is a young tree and its root system is not firmly established. That doesn't mean that something was wrong with the tree when it was planted. It was the storm that damaged the tree. However, with some careful attention and nurturing, that tree can in time stand tall, grow, and produce healthy fruit.

You are not a mistake. *Nothing about you is a mistake.* The abuse you endured may have bent you, but you were not *born* broken. You have great value and purpose.

How priceless is your unfailing love, O God! People take
refuge in the shadow of your wings.

Psalm 36:7 (NIV)

Chapter Five

The Root of Codependency

When trees are planted too close together, their roots become intertwined. They compete for resources. The closeness limits their growth potential and threatens their health. They aren't able to produce as many leaves or as much fruit as a tree that has more room to grow. Instead of expanding wide and flourishing, the trees grow tall and skinny—a pale, sickly shadow of what they were designed to be. When we become too closely intertwined with others, depending on them to provide our sense of value and purpose, we can also experience similar damaging effects to our personal growth and development. This is often known as codependency.

We are born into this world with basic needs. As we discussed in Chapter Two, we need our parents or caregivers to provide love, nurturing, support, and acceptance. Our sense of identity is developed in childhood. These vital anchors help us feel secure enough to take risks, make mistakes, and explore and discover our own unique desires, skills, qualities, and talents. That security also helps us to bounce back from failures and learn more about ourselves in the process. A healthy parent or caregiver encourages age-appropriate degrees of independence, enabling us to progressively gain insight and confidence in who we are.

If you had a parent(s) with an addiction; a mental, emotional, or physical illness, or simple self-centeredness, you most likely didn't receive a solid, healthy foundation for self-discovery. You may have been given the message early on that your feelings, needs, and desires were unimportant or secondary to your parent's. When you expressed your wants and needs, you may have even been made to feel dismissed, selfish, or guilty.[1] In some cases, the parent-child roles were reversed. You carried the weight of responsibilities you weren't equipped to handle as a child. This may have been necessary for your emotional or physical survival. For example, if you had an alcoholic parent, you may have had to make meals and/or take care of siblings from a very young age. Maybe your parent was in an abusive or dysfunctional relationship and heavily depended on you for support or comfort. Patterns of consistently rescuing or caring for your parent may have developed.

Or, perhaps you had a parent who made you feel that the only way you could be accepted, loved, or "good enough" for them was to suppress your own thoughts, needs, opinions, and desires. We have a strong and natural desire for our parents' approval, so we learn to adapt our behavior and expressions to their preferences and standards.

Can you relate?

These childhood messages and experiences can cause us to link our acceptance, purpose, and value to our ability to care for others physically and/or emotionally, make others happy, and gain their approval. This can follow us into adulthood, leading us to sacrifice and accommodate others in ways that are draining and destructive—to us and to them as well. Yet the driving need to feel self-worth, purpose, and value runs so deep that we are often willing to sacrifice our physical, mental, and emotional health in order to meet it.

Sadly, our "helping" isn't true helping at all. It often actually protects others from experiencing the consequences of their choices, further enabling and encouraging them to continue in those damaging patterns. We become so enmeshed with someone else that we mold our behavior and opinions to fit what they seem to want or need, preventing us from discovering who we truly are and what we have to offer, independent of our performance or success at "fixing" or pleasing others.

Codependency can cause us to unconsciously be drawn to those who are similar to our parent(s). We look for others who we can help, rescue, and "fix" in order to continue to fill our ongoing need to feel valuable and important. The codependent's draw to "needy" people means that we often find ourselves in draining or abusive one-sided relationships. We often think of people with codependency entering into romantic relationships with those with alcoholism or other addictions. While that is true, unhealthy self-sacrifice can exhibit itself in all types of relationships—romantic, friendships, parental, and/or working relationships.

In healthy relationships, there is a natural "give-and-take." Over time, both people in the relationship provide and receive a relatively balanced degree of love, support, and understanding. This beneficial bond promotes individual growth, strength, and a sense of resilience. At the same time, each person has a very clear sense of their own identity, value, and purpose separate from the other person. In a codependent relationship, each person has his/her dysfunctional role. One person is the "taker" and plays the victim role, while the other person is the "giver," willing to sacrifice their own well-being in order to please the other person.[2] In other words, one person creates the chaos and the other person cleans it up.

We may think it's because we love or care about the other person, but it's a distorted form of love. In truth, if we are really honest with ourselves, we may love the sense of worth and identity caring for the person gives us more than we love the person. The codependent needs to be needed. We twist ourselves into a pretzel—changing our behavior and our personalities—in order to try to make the other person happy. While maintaining the relationship may damage, exhaust, and frustrate us, we are hesitant to do anything to risk losing it. Our value and purpose is far too tangled up and invested in its survival.

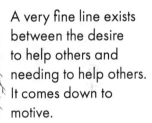

A very fine line exists between the desire to help others and needing to help others. It comes down to motive.

Barking up the wrong tree

A very fine line exists between the desire to help others and needing to help others. In our experience, it comes down to motive. Why do you want to help others? Is it because you genuinely have their best interests at heart? Or is the goal to gain their approval or make you feel good about yourself? Is it necessary for you to feel valuable? Maybe investing in someone else is your way of avoiding taking risks and learning how to live and thrive independently. If the answer is more about filling a need in *you*—for recognition, value, control, or security—than in helping the other person, you may be codependent. **From our personal and clinical experience, other symptoms of codependency include:**

- **Low Self-Esteem.** When we rely on others' feelings about us for our sense of value, we will always feel insecure about ourselves. People's feelings and opinions of us are notoriously unreliable, often misguided, and based on incomplete information or their own wounds or self-serving motives.

- **"Chameleon" like behavior.** If our worth is tied to how others need or feel about us, we will adapt or suppress our own feelings, thoughts, and opinions to be accepted or loved by the other person. As a result, we often don't even know what we enjoy, like, or feel.

- **Assuming the role of rescuer or problem solver.** We take care of the other person. Since taking care of or "fixing" someone else is the source of our value, we often make excuses for the other person's inappropriate or irresponsible behavior.

- **Difficulty setting boundaries or saying "no"** even if it negatively impacts your physical, mental, and emotional health. This is often referred to as "people pleasing."

- **Suppressing our own needs and feelings** in order not to upset the other person. We feel guilty for thinking about ourselves and our needs. However, over time, we often become angry and resentful toward the other person. Our needs and desires are too strong to be suppressed indefinitely.

Unravel the Root
Debbie's Truth Story

State the facts.

After the painful demise of yet another romantic relationship, Debbie was at a crossroads. She had sacrificed over and over again to try to make each man happy, but the outcome was always the same: She felt deeply hurt, exhausted, and abandoned. She began to wonder, *Why does every relationship I have end this way?* Finding the answer to that question became her primary focus.

Debbie began to see how this painful pattern had negatively impacted her daughters' view of men, relationships, and marriage. She didn't want to keep hurting the people she loved. She couldn't keep making the same mistakes. The emotional pain had become too overwhelming. She began a year of counseling and intensive studies at her church that focused on healing from codependency and dysfunctional relationships.

Slowly, the roots of Debbie's choices began to emerge. She grew up believing her parents and their marriage was pretty close to perfect. During her early years, everything seemed stable and happy. Still, as the middle child in a large family, she struggled to find her place and purpose. She didn't know where she "fit." What she *did* know was that she was her father's favorite. Debbie longed to make him happy and proud of her.

When Debbie was 12 years old, the "perfect" exterior of her parents' marriage shattered and Debbie's father decided to leave the family. The day before he left, he shared the news of his leaving with Debbie before anyone else in the family—including her mother. After her father left, she missed him terribly and continually tried to reach out to him. But he distanced himself from the family and repeatedly broke promises to her. The value and approval she felt as her father's confidante and favorite suddenly evaporated.

After the divorce, her mother worked constantly to keep the family afloat financially. Debbie found purpose in assuming primary responsibility for caring for her two younger brothers. Through her recovery process, Debbie realized that for her whole life she was trying to find value in and approval from men—first from her father and then by caring for her brothers.

Debbie realized she was looking to create the "perfect family" that she thought she had growing up. Since she found purpose and value in the role of confidante and caretaker, she unconsciously chose men who needed "rescuing." With each relationship, Debbie committed to do whatever dance seemed to make him happy and make her feel loved. But she never was able to achieve that result. As each relationship ended, her sense of self-worth and value diminished. She was determined to get it right the next time. Her sense of who she was depended on "fixing" and caring for and being loved by the men in her life. Through her healing process, Debbie realized that these men didn't leave her because she wasn't valuable. Their own issues made them incapable of exhibiting the selfless, unconditional love she craved.

The more Debbie connected with her faith and church community, the more she felt accepted and loved for who she truly is. Although she's experienced a great deal of healing, she's not sure she trusts her judgment in relationships yet. But she knows now that she doesn't have to be a caregiver or in a relationship to have value and purpose.

Let's review: Debbie wondered why all of her relationships ended the same way. A "daddy's girl" who believed her family life was pretty ideal, Debbie was devastated when her father left the family when she was 12 years old. To fill the void he left in her heart, Debbie found purpose and worth in caring for her younger brothers. As she got older, she continued to try to find love and value in caring for men and making them happy.

Let's reflect: What facts of your story are similar to Debbie's?

In what ways are the facts of your story different?

How can you relate to Debbie's feelings even if the facts of your story are not the same?

Expose the lie.

Debbie's value as a child was tied to being "daddy's girl." When he rejected her, she tried to find her love and value in caring for and rescuing men. These were the lies Debbie wove around her facts: "Why would my own father reject me? Why wasn't I enough for him to stay? Why did he stop loving me? Something must be wrong with me."

Let's reflect: In what ways did you tie your value to others' views and acceptance of you?

If you experienced rejection, what lies did you tell yourself about your worth?

Acknowledge the behavior.

Since Debbie tied her value to the role of caretaker and was desperate to find the love she lost when her father abandoned her, she was drawn to men who she could "rescue."

Let's reflect: What insight does this give you as you consider some of your own behaviors and choices?

Embrace the truth.

Looking back, Debbie could see how both of her parents came from wealthy families, where they were expected to act a certain way and project a certain image. That pattern of maintaining a false, perfect image in order to be accepted was then repeated and passed down to Debbie and her siblings.

Let's reflect: After reading this chapter and Debbie's story, what roots of people pleasing or codependency, if any, do you recognize in your family history?

Debbie realized that her father most likely left because it became too painful and exhausting to project a "perfect" image that didn't reflect the reality of his life. It wasn't because Debbie wasn't worthy of his love. She also realized that she felt like she had been abandoned by every man in her life. She wondered what was wrong with her. She tried to do everything she could to be lovable and self-sacrificing and was still rejected.

Through the healing process, she realized that all these men left or rejected her for reasons that had nothing to do with her. As she distanced herself from unhealthy relationships, Debbie began to blossom. She began to discover what she liked and didn't like, her hidden dreams, gifts, and desires. She had deeply buried them over the years as she tried to conform and meet others' needs and expectations. Debbie now embraces who she is and continues to discover new, surprising things about herself.

Let's reflect: As Debbie began to seek help, she identified the root, lie, and truth of her story. In the columns below, write the root, lie, and truth of your story of codependency.

ROOT	LIE	TRUTH
Debbie's dad left the family. Debbie was forced to care for her siblings. Debbie found her worth in taking care of others.	*Debbie believed she wasn't important. Debbie believed her value was in helping others. Debbie needed to be needed.*	*Debbie's dad left because of his own issues. Being codependent was robbing Debbie of finding who she really is.* ***Debbie has a purpose.***

Change your choices.

Through counseling and connecting more deeply with her faith, Debbie has been set free from depending on men for her worth. She understands that she has value and is worthy of being loved for who she is. It's not dependent on her performance or rescuing others. She is finding her joy—but not her value—in serving her church and spending time with and caring for her children and grandchildren. She is open to marrying again, but her worth no longer depends on it.

Let's reflect: What habits and behaviors rooted in codependency do you need and want to change?

What is one step you can take *right now* to discover who you truly are, separate from relationships? (Examples: Read a book on codependency or go to a movie, have dinner, or take a vacation by yourself.)

Free to flourish

One of the most devastating consequences of codependency is that because we are so focused on being who others want us to be, we miss out on discovering who *we* are. We miss out on our own personal, individual journey of self-discovery and development. That journey is the one where we learn what we enjoy, where we discover our talents, gifts, and qualities that we missed because we are too busy taking care of others. We miss walking out the plan and purpose for which we were created. And those around us miss out, too.

Finding that path to who we really are requires us to face hard truths about ourselves. We may have to admit that all of our "helping" is really more about *us* than about *them*. We may have to acknowledge that the people who we want so much to love us actually aren't healthy enough to be capable of it. Those realizations can rock our world. But as the truth is exposed, the light can shine in. When we let go of pursuing relationships, performance, and "rescuing" as our source of value, we begin to discover the *real* us—the one buried beneath all that caretaking and enabling.

And trust us, we are of immense value. *We* are worth discovering.

I praise you because I am fearfully and wonderfully made;
your works are wonderful, I know that full well.

Psalm 139:14 (NIV)

Keep Growing!

A seed of encouragement

From the time I was 15 years old, I was never without a boyfriend. I shifted my choices, opinions, and preferences to whatever I thought would make men want me, whatever I thought would make them happy. When one relationship ended, I looked for my next "fix." I needed men's approval to feel beautiful and worthwhile. In Chapter Five, you read Debbie's Truth Story. Debbie's story is much like my mother's. My own mother's long history of failed relationships profoundly affected my life and my view of men. Our relationship was strained and rocky as I entered young adulthood. I felt like she was giving me relationship advice that she had never followed herself. But she is also the person who helped lead me to and continues to walk me through my healing.

When I was pregnant with my second child, my marriage—and my self-esteem—crumbled. My pregnancy prevented me from running to another man. I was forced, for the first time, to be alone long enough to reflect on why my relationships always ended so badly. At the same time, I was watching my mom take steps to get healthier. She was still in an unhealthy relationship, but it was clear that her choices and mindsets were changing. So when my marriage was struggling, I reached out to her. And she was there for me. She didn't try to give me advice. She simply said, "What do you need from me?" That love and acceptance was pivotal for me.

I had some knowledge of God; but for the first time, I began to truly pour out my issues and problems to Him instead of looking to another man to make me feel valuable. I also went to a counselor who asked some hard questions that challenged me to consider why I missed the "red flags" in so many of the men that I had dated. At first I was defensive, but I gradually realized how I kept missing obvious warning signs. I began to see how my identity was so wrapped up in meeting men's wants and needs that I didn't even know who I was.

Through that process and finding support through my church, I began to understand how I was repeating the patterns of my childhood. My upbringing had profoundly affected my view of men, of myself, and my view of God as Father. As I began to forgive, my relationship with God began to grow stronger and deeper. My relationship with my mother also began to heal. At times, this was an extremely challenging, painful journey. But it has been worth every step.

As I let go of looking to men for my value, I began to discover who I am. I began to explore what I liked and found my purpose. The internal battle between being who I am and who I thought others wanted me to be has ceased. I have the peace of living an authentic life. While I'm compassionate toward others and their struggles, I no longer feel responsible for "fixing" them because my identity is no longer tied to others. The people in my life now are positive and want to grow, too. They challenge me to continue to grow.

I used to run away to a new man or a new distraction to avoid taking a hard look at my choices and behaviors. But when I finally quit running, I found someone valuable and beautiful, someone I grew to love: *Me*.

—Lisa Rowe, LCSW

Chapter Six

Where Do I Grow Now?

By now, we are hoping you are feeling unraveled in a good way. That your eyes have been opened to the reasons behind the choices you've made and the destructive cycles you've been trying so hard to break. And we acknowledge that you may also be feeling unraveled in a vulnerable way. A little bit at loose ends. You know the "why" now, but you don't fully know the way. The way forward. *How do you move forward into a new way of living? What does that look like? Can your life really be different? Are you really strong enough?*

Healing comes in layers. We encourage you to get connected with a local support group or church community.

Each of us—Karin, Melinda, and Lisa—at different times and in different ways, have been at this very same crossroads. Feeling weak, weary, inadequate, and weighed down in our dysfunction. In fact, we have been and will be at this place numerous times throughout our lives. Change and growth is an ongoing journey. Healing comes in layers. The best news we can possibly leave you with is this: You *do not* have to do this alone. You weren't *meant* to do this alone. We encourage you to get connected with a local support group or church community. We have been greatly inspired and stretched through our personal relationship with God and our continually growing relationships with others who are positive and encouraging. God Himself wants to walk alongside you in this new journey. We can't end our time together without sharing with you about Him because He has made all the difference in our journeys. This book is the fruit of the healing God has done in each of our lives. We didn't earn it. We were just desperate for a love that would never leave us. In that desperation, each of us, in our own way, cried out, "God, show me more of Who You are. If You really love me, if You're really there, show me a better way." *And He did.*

That's a prayer we believe God longs to answer. In our experience, a real relationship with God always starts with a sense of His love. Knowing we're loved is essential to trust. God doesn't just want us to have a "better" life. He wants us to have a relationship with Him. But it's our *choice*. Often it's a choice we make when we are out of other options. For Karin, it was when she realized that sex and substances could not numb her pain or fill the longing in her soul for unconditional love and acceptance. For Melinda, the moment came when she had exhausted all her efforts to earn God's love, "fix" her family, and heal her tortured mind and ailing body. For Lisa, that moment came when she found herself pregnant and realized that the marriage she had fought so hard to save was literally crumbling before her eyes, along with her shaky self-esteem. Someone bigger than ourselves was going to have to show each of us a better way. Sure, it was risky. But we were just desperate enough to take the risk. We are different people because of experiencing God's love. Real love didn't magically change our circumstances, but it did radically change our perspective. It empowered us to keep walking when it was hard and heavy because we knew the journey was being led with love. A continual, close, and loving relationship with God is the only choice that brought us peace and lasting fruit.

God's love didn't magically change our circumstances, but it did radically change our perspective.

We have additional resources in the back of this book if you're interested in learning more about how to pursue this journey of faith that has made all the difference for us.

Embrace the journey

You're at a crossroads. Which way will *you* go? A new path *is* risky. We warned you about that from the very beginning of this book. Be patient with the process. Be kind to yourself. You didn't get here overnight. You won't establish healthier habits and patterns overnight either. There will be ups and downs. It's going to be tremendously hard at times. There will be days when you feel like you're making no progress at all. Some people may fight to keep you in unhealthy patterns because it's in *their* best interest. It allows them to continue in *their* unhealthy patterns. You'll feel like giving up. You'll try to convince yourself it's not worth it.

Take it from three women who have been walking this new path out for quite a few years now: It *is* worth it. Change—even good change—feels scary and unpredictable, but it will get *easier*. Choices that seem so hard at first will eventually become a natural way of living. No matter what your past looks like or how many mistakes you've made, growing new, healthier fruit *is* possible. One choice at a time. One step at a time.

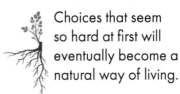

Choices that seem so hard at first will eventually become a natural way of living.

Remember this: Your journey up to this point has just led to more pain. This *new* journey will also be painful and difficult. But here's the key difference: The pain of this *new* journey has a beautiful purpose. One step at a time you can now walk toward a healthier, freer place. You will be leaving a healthier legacy for your family, community, and world. You will inspire others around you, too. Share this book with them. Share your journey. The path is always sweeter with encouraging fellow travelers.

Whatever you give up or lose along this new pathway, you will gain much, much more in return. Which way will *you* go? It's your choice. May your journey be fruitful. We're rooting for you.

"I am the vine; you are the branches. If you remain in me and I in you, you will bear much fruit . . . "

John 15:4-5 (NIV)

Resources

Alcoholics Anonymous (AA)
212-870-3400 | https://www.aa.org

Narcotics Anonymous (NA)
818-773-9999 | https://www.na.org

Support After Abortion (SAA)
844-289-HOPE (4673) | https://www.supportafterabortion.com

Overeaters Anonymous (OA)
505-891-2664 | https://oa.org

National Eating Disorders Association
800-931-2237 | https://www.nationaleatingdisorders.org

National Suicide Prevention Lifeline
800-273-8255 | https://suicidepreventionlifeline.org

National Domestic Violence Hotline
800-799-7233 | https://www.thehotline.org

RAINN: Rape, Abuse, Incest National Network
800-656-4673 | https://www.rainn.org

Childhelp National Child Abuse Hotline
800-422-4453 | https://www.childhelp.org/hotline/

The National Center on Elder Abuse
855-500-3537 | https://ncea.acl.gov

Co-Dependents Anonymous
888-444-2359 | http://coda.org

Lifetime Adoption Hotline
800-923-6784 | https://lifetimeadoption.com

National Alliance on Mental Illness
800-950-6264 | https://www.nami.org"

National Human Trafficking Hotline
888-373-7888 Text 233733 | https://humantraffickinghotline.org

Grief Resource Network
828-726-9554 | https://griefresourcenetwork.com/crisis-center/hotlines/

Grief Anonymous
https://griefanonymous.com

American Pregnancy Helpline - Miscarriages
866-942-6466 | http://www.thehelpline.org/

National Problem Gambling Helpline
800-522-4700 | https://www.ncpgambling.org/

Sex Addicts Anonymous
800-477-8191 | https://saa-recovery.org

Crisis Text Line
Text 741741 | https://www.crisistextline.org

Christian Broadcasting Network with the 700 Club Prayer Line
800-700-7000 | https://www1.cbn.com/prayer

Joy FM Prayer Line
877-800-7729 | http://florida.thejoyfm.com/

Trinity Broadcasting Network Prayer Line
888-731-1000 | https://tbn.org/

Daystar Prayer Line
800-329-0029

Breakthrough Prayer Line
800-424-8644

Life Outreach International Prayer Line
800-947-5433 | https://lifetoday.org/

Morris Cerullo Prayer Line
866-756-4200 | https://mcwe.com/

Crossroads Prayer Line
866-273-4444 | http://www.crossroads.ca

Family Broadcasting Corporation Prayer Line
800-365-3732 | https://familybroadcastingcorporation.com/

Endnotes

Chapter 2

1   Inge Bretherton, "The Origins of Attachment Theory: John Bowlby and Mary Ainsworth." *Developmental Psychology* 28, no.5 (September 1992): 759-775.

2   *Merriam-Webster, s.v.* "abandon," accessed January 2, 2020, https://www.merriam-webster.com/dictionary/abandon.

Chapter 3

1   "What is Addiction?" American Psychiatric Association, accessed January 16, 2020, https://www.psychiatry.org/patients-families/addiction/what-is-addiction.

2   ibid.

3   Elizabeth Hartney, BSc., MSc., MA, PhD, "An Overview of Behavioral Addiction," Very Well Mind (website), accessed January 4, 2020, https://www.verywellmind.com/addictive-behaviors-4157291.

4   ibid.

5   "What is Substance Abuse?" WebMD, accessed February 14, 2020, https://www.webmd.com/mental-health/addiction/substance-abuse#1.

6   Marina Barnard and Joy Barlow, "Discovering Parental Drug Dependence: Silence and Disclosure." *Children and Society* 17, no. 1 (2003): 45 - 56. https://onlinelibrary.wiley.com/doi/abs/10.1002/chi.727.

7   J. M. Solis, J. M. Shadur, A.R. Burns and A. M. Hussong, "Understanding the Diverse Needs of Children Whose Parents Abuse Substances." *Current Drug Abuse Reviews* 5, no. 2 (June 2012): 135–147. https://www.ncbi.nlm.nih.gov/pmc/articles/PMC3676900/.

8   Tian Dayton, MA, PhD, TEP, "The Set Up: Living with Addiction (curriculum)," accessed December 30, 2019: 4-5. http://www.nacoa. net/pdfs/The%20Set%20Up%20for%20Social%20Work%20 Curriculum.pdf.

9   Timothy W. Fong, MD, "Understanding and Managing Compulsive Sexual Behaviors." *Psychiatry* (Edgmont) 3, no.11 (November 2006): 51–58. https://www.ncbi.nlm.nih.gov/pmc/articles/PMC2945841.

10 Carolyn C. Ross, MD, MPH, "Overexposed and Under-prepared: The Effects of Early Exposure to Sexual Content," Psychology Today, August 13, 2012, https://www.psychologytoday.com/us/blog/real-heal-ing/201208/overexposed-and-under-prepared-the-effects-early-expo-sure-sexual-content.

11 *Merriam-Webster, s.v.* "pornography," accessed December 28, 2019, https://www.merriam-webster.com/dictionary/pornography.

12 Edie Weinstein, MSW, LSW, "Growing Up Too Fast: Early Exposure to Sex," Psych Central, July 8, 2018, https://psychcentral.com/blog/ growing-up-too-fast-early-exposure-to-sex/.

13 "The Impact of Adult Infidelity on Children," Two of Us, accessed January 20, 2020, https://www.twoofus.org/educational-content/ articles/the-impact-of-adult-infidelity-on-children/.

14 Libby Lyons, MSW, LCSW, CEDS, "Understanding the Differences between Food Addictions and an Eating Disorder." Eating Disorder Hope, accessed December 28, 2019, https://www.eatingdisorderhope. com/blog/food-addictions-eating-disorder.

15 *Pooh's Grand Adventure: The Search for Christopher Robin*. Directed by Karl Geurs. United States: Walt Disney Video Premiere, 1997.

Chapter 4

1   "Effects of Domestic Violence on Children," Office on Women's Health, accessed February 13, 2020, https://www.womenshealth.gov/relationships-and-safety/domestic-violence/effects-domestic-violence-children.

2   "Preventing Emotional Abuse," Prevent Child Abuse America, accessed December 30, 2019, https://preventchildabuse.org/resource/preventing-emotional-abuse/.

3   Steven Kairys, MD, MPH, Charles F. Johnson, MD and the Committee on Child Abuse and Neglect, "The Psychological Maltreatment of Children—Technical Report." *Pediatrics, Official Journal of the American Academy of Pediatrics* 109; e68 (April 2002). https://doi.org/10.1542/peds.109.4.e68.

4   World Health Organization and International Society for Prevention of Child Abuse and Neglect, *Preventing Child Maltreatment: A Guide to Taking Action and Generating Evidence*, (Geneva: WHO Press, 2006), 10.

5   *American Psychological Association, s.v.* "Sexual Abuse," accessed December 30, 2019, https://www.apa.org/topics/sexual-abuse/index.

Chapter 5

1   Leon Seltzer, Ph.D, "Codependent or Simply Dependent: What's the Big Difference?" Psychology Today, December 11, 2014, https://www.psychologytoday.com/us/blog/evolution-the-self/201412/codependent-or-simply-dependent-what-s-the-big-difference.

2   Carly Breit, "You May Be In a Codependent Relationship. Here's How to Overcome It," Time, August 2, 2018, https://time.com/5349927/codependent-relationship-signs/.

Made in the USA
Columbia, SC
31 January 2023

11344126R00052